The Wome to Fitness

A Spiritual and Practical Way

By Audrey Muhammad

Based on the book How to Eat to Live

The Women's Guide to Fitness. Copyright 2023 by Audrey Muhammad. All rights reserved. Printed in the United States of America. No part of this book may be reproduced or transmitted in any form or by any means, electronic or mechanical, including photocopying, recording, or by any information storage and retrieval system, without written permission from the publisher.
For more information, contact by email: audrey.a.muhammad@gmail.com

As-Salaam Alaikum.
(May Peace Be Upon You.)

Author's Note

This information is shared with the understanding that you accept complete responsibility for your health and wellbeing. The results of any techniques suggested herein cannot always be anticipated and never guaranteed. Not all exercises or diets are suitable for everyone. You should have your physician's permission before you begin any exercise or dietary program. The instructions and advice presented in this book are in no way intended as a substitute for medical advice. The author and distributors of this book disclaim any liability or loss in connection with the exercise program and advice herein.

Dedication

This book is dedicated to my beautiful sisters of the M.G.T. & G.C.C and the GOD that made us.

Special thanks to:

- My sister, Broyny, and my father, Ernest Flowers for their Illustrations;
- My mother, Eva Flowers, for her love and support (May God be pleased with her);
- My brother, Vincent, who encouraged me to write this book;
- My supportive sister-in-law, Nkenge, for her objective input
- Sister Nina Muhammad for taking some of the initial photos included in this book;
- My daughter, Hasana, for taking photos and revising the layout of the book;
- And the divine example of The Honorable Minister Louis Farrakhan, whose lecture "God's Healing Power," was a motivating factor in me creating this book.

I thank God for you all.

Table of Contents

Chapter Title	**Page**
Purpose	6
Chapter – 1 Faith and Prayer	8
Chapter – 2 Goal Setting	9
Chapter – 3 Nutrition	11
Chapter – 4 The Fasting Foundation	13
Chapter – 5 Brain Health And Dis-ease	15
Chapter – 6 Energize With Exercise	16
Chapter – 7 Recommendations and References	31

Purpose

The purpose of this little book is to remind us, as sisters, of one statement made by Master Fard Muhammad:

"I can sit on top of the world and tell everyone that the most beautiful Nation is in the wilderness of North America. But do not let me catch any sister other than herself in regards to living the life and weighing properly."

What life is being referenced here? He wants us to live the life of a Muslim, a righteous life. A life where we are submitting our will to do the will of Allah (God) and seek refuge in him and only him, and not in food, drugs, etc. (We will discuss that later.)

Lastly, he mentions weighing properly. What does the word "weigh" mean? "Weigh" is a verb that means to consider or balance in the mind. It also means to burden or oppress. "Properly" is an adverb which means "suitably" or "appropriately." When we weigh "other" or different from ourselves, we have put on a "burden" that Allah doesn't want us to bear. In the lecture by The Honorable Minister Farrakhan entitled "God's Healing Power," he spoke of God's hatred of fat. He mentioned that The Honorable Elijah Muhammad said that the beauty of our appearance is in our weight. The fatter we get, the more we take away from the beauty of our appearance and we also tend to look older. Have you ever noticed how easy it was for Oprah Winfrey to play a woman twice her age in the movie "The Color Purple?" Her weight, at the time, made her look older. [Keep in mind, the essence of our beauty is in our ability to submit to Allah.}

Excess physical weight holds us down and makes our bodies ugly, distorted and most of all, unhealthy. Negative mental weight or "burdens" do the same thing. It holds us down (meaning we are not productive), and it makes us unattractive and unhealthy. Why? Because negative dispositions or funky attitudes are not beautiful. They are downright ugly. Believe me, I've been "there" and I'm working on not doing "that."

In essence Sisters, we want to weigh properly and be "fit" to live the life of a Muslim. According to the Random House Unabridged Dictionary, "fit" means adapted or suited, appropriate, proper or becoming qualified or competent". The suffix "ness" denotes a quality or state. Thus, we have the word "fitness" which means, "being in a state of health". In biology, "fitness" refers to genetic contribution and the ability of a population to maintain or increase its numbers in succeeding generations. If we do not first improve our minds to improve our diets and bodies, we will not produce a healthy generation.

In order for us to fulfill this vision Master Fard has for us to be the most beautiful nation, we must truly believe it. Nevertheless, we know that belief accounts for nothing unless it is carried into practice. Chapter 1 addresses faith and prayer, the first things we must learn to practice.

The Women's Guide to Fitness
By Audrey Muhammad

Dr. Audrey Muhammad, is an educator, AFAA Certified Group Fitness Instructor and NASM Certified Women's Fitness Specialist who uses her martial arts experience and knowledge of exercise to motivate and educate sisters on practical ways to lose weight and stay fit.

Her book incorporates the diet *How to Eat to Live* and includes chapters on fasting, prayer, goal setting, and nutrition. An easy-to-learn exercise routine with detailed photo examples is also included. The author uses a fun-loving, "sisterly voice" and humor to point out how people rationalize ("use rational lies") to justify eating too much, too often and not exercising. This little book is easy to follow and thoroughly enjoyable.

"The Sister's Guide to Fitness is a motivating and informative guide to reclaiming physical health. A Must Read!"
-Dr. Nkenge Jackson, OBGYN, Savannah, GA

"It should be mandatory reading material for MGT sisters and sisters in general. The book makes you feel better. It has scripture and solution for my spiritual and physical wellbeing. The workout in the book is fantastic!"
-Mary Muhammad, Richmond, CA (mother of two children)

For a Get Fit To Live Workshop in your city, contact audrey.a.muhammad@gmail.com

Chapter 1

Faith and Prayer

In the Holy Quran, chapter 40:60, it says, *"And you Lord says: Pray to Me, I will answer you"*.

Have we asked Allah(God) to help us lose weight? We are talking about the Lord of the Worlds. Do we doubt that he can perform such a small feat as giving us the willpower to improve our diets and strengthen our desire to exercise? Actually, desire is the key. Desire feeds the will. If we don't desire anything, we are not praying because we don't have any goals. We have too much doubt and not enough faith in Allah's power to change our condition. However, we must remember that Allah(God) will not change our condition until we change our hearts. As my mother used to say, "God helps those who help themselves."

Some of us may think, "Hey, I wear my weight well," as if the excess baggage was a beautiful garment. I am not talking about us just loving ourselves or our "big beautiful self." I am talking about being fit, being healthy. Excess fat is not healthy. I know we all are not made to be 120 pounds, however, it is a good guideline for us.

Pray to Allah (God) to help guide you in your endeavor to exercise and be fit. Notice that I didn't say "exercise and lose weight." Sisters, some of us are skinny, but we are weak. We have no "power behind the punch," no strength in our stride, and no conviction in our conversation. Pray to Allah to be fit, and then go to work. Be and it is.

Chapter 2

Goal Setting

In the early 1990s, I was blessed with the opportunity to visit an M.G.T. class in Denver, Colorado. In attendance were quite a few elder sisters who were in the Nation when the Messenger was among us. One elderly sister gave a brief, but profound presentation. She shared with the sisters that at one point in time, she was under great distress because all the sisters around her were getting married and she was still single. She wrote to the Messenger of her plight and pleaded with him to tell her what she could do. The Messenger, of course, responded. According to the sister, he wrote back to her simply this: *"Dear Sister, Know thyself. Your Brother and Servant, Elijah Muhammad."*

He apparently wanted her to have a goal in life, to decide what she wanted besides a husband. We all have a purpose for which we are put on this earth. Once we find that purpose and we are in submission to Allah(God), we are happy and experience joy in spite of the trials and tribulations of life. Why? Because we are on the most exciting journey of all-the journey to know self. On the tape, "The Mind Of God", by Minister Farrakhan, he asked the question, "Why do we do what we do?" Our main goal in losing or maintaining our weight should be for health reasons. A beautiful body is just the wonderful by-product. Suggestions for setting goals include the following:

1. **Decide what you want.** (Also ask yourself, "Why?" so that you can be sure your goal is properly motivated.)

2. **What will you need to get what you want, what resources, etc.** (ex. Do I need a gym membership? Do I need to reduce the amount of food I eat?)

3. **What type of commitment do I need to have?** (Studies show that it takes at least 21 days to end one habitat and form a new one. Commit to a workout plan for at least 21 days. You will love the difference in the way you look and feel.

4. **Write down your goals and what is the first step you need to take in order to achieve your goal?** (Writing your goals down somehow makes the reality of the goal more tangible. It becomes something you can see.)

5. **Prioritize your goals.** Divide them into daily, weekly, monthly, and yearly goals. (The yearly goals should consist of 1-3 years, 3-5 years, and 5-10 years.)

6. <u>**Pray**</u> and <u>**visualize**</u> **your goal becoming a reality.** How will you look and feel? Believe it! Feel it! See it! (Pray for Allah's Blessings)

7. **Take action.** Choose an action you can do immediately to take one step toward achieving your goal. A 23-year-old sister told me that she wanted to learn how to drive. I told her that when she really desires to learn, she will. She responded by

saying, "I do desire it." "No," I said. "Once you truly desire it, you will take action. She finally agreed because she recalled how she would make up excuses for why her mother or brother wouldn't be able to help her. She wants a license, but presently doesn't desire one. A want is a feeling of need. A desire impels you to action. (Always pray like God has to do it all and then work like you have to do it all.

Chapter 3

Nutrition

How to eat to live. Need I say more? Of course, we wouldn't be in the predicament we are in if we truly practiced how to eat to live. Yes, we can gain weight even if we are eating one meal a day, but are we exercising? A better question would be, "How many meals are we eating in our one meal a day?"

My sister once told me, "You may not eat pig, but you eat like a pig." At first, my mouth fell open in shock, and then I looked at my huge second plate full of vegetable fried rice. I soon became ashamed because I was even thinking about getting a third plate. I love food. However, I know I would be fat if I didn't love exercise even more. Nevertheless, I soon realized that it was becoming harder to keep the pounds off, even if exercising if I continued to eat the amount I was eating and what I was eating. Would you believe I could easily eat an entire bean pie? That was for an appetizer.

The Honorable Elijah Muhammad has two wonderful books we need to read and read again: How To Eat To Live Book I and How To Eat Live Book II. We need to dust these "lost books" of the Nation off and practice them. Have we forgotten that the caption of the book says "From God In Person - Master Fard Muhammad?" This alone should encourage us not to take it lightly. In the books, the Honorable Elijah Muhammad said the best foods are navy beans, whole wheat bread(toasted), and pure milk. This divine combination will sufficiently provide us with needed protein, fiber, and calories. Fruit, of course, makes a nice dessert. The bean pie is also a good dessert, but don't eat the entire pie in one sitting (smile).

Keep in mind that a vegetarian diet is best because of its high water content, which is more in line with the composition of our best and is more calming. In the book As A Woman Thinketh, it says a woman with pure thoughts no longer desires impure food. The psychological effects of a vegetarian diet are wonderful. You will be surprised at how you are less likely to lose your temper once you eliminate these "aggressive" meats from your diet.

Oftentimes, we become emotional eaters. We eat hoping to feel better emotionally and not for the nutritional benefits. Why are we still hungry after eating a bag of potato chips? Our body hasn't received the nutrients it needs and desires so our stomach "computer" screen says, "Malnutrition! Input more food please!" You will also be less likely to seek refuge in your rolls and rice once you improve your diet and exercise. Notice that I didn't use diet as a verb. Diet as a verb implies a temporary change of your eating pattern as in: "I'm going to diet." Your diet(noun) is, overall, what you eat to sustain and maintain your lean body. Instead of dieting, let's improve our diet by first practicing how to eat to live. How many of us have eaten a slice of bean pie at night because we "forgot" to eat our dessert earlier or eat everything in sight because we plan to fast the next day?" Say, "Never again, never again." Let us eat to live, and not live to eat.

Chapter 4

The Fasting Foundation

How would you like to virtually eliminate many illnesses from your life?

> "Fasting is one of the greatest "doctors" we have. FAST! It cleans the impurities out of the blood and causes the body to eliminate the poison stored in it from previous meals--sometimes from previous meals of many years, as the folds in our intestines can carry particles of food for a long time, and holds strength enough in them to keep us alive for two months." (How To Eat Live, The Honorable Elijah Muhammad.)

Sisters, how many of us practice the National Fast? National Fast? What's that? (Some may ask.) In October of 1988, Minister Louis Farrakhan instituted a monthly three-day fast that would begin on the first Thursday of each month after the evening meal. This fast, when practiced, helps to cultivate a peaceful unity among the believers and the sisterhood. Sisters can go out and have tea together after M.G.T. class as they encourage one another to continue the fast. There is definitely strength in numbers. It's motivating to be around fasting Muslims. Make sure you are one of them.

In Study Guide #12, it states, "Fasting in the right spirit helps us display repentance. We must be of humble spirit so that we may show Allah(God) that we are sick/sorry over all that we have done to offend Him."

You will feel absolutely wonderful after a three-day fast, especially if you eat healthy (no sweets and fried foods) a couple of days before your fast. Remember, "O, you who believe, fasting is prescribed for you, as it was prescribed for those before you, so that you may guard against evil." (Holy Quran 2:183). (Keep in mind, if you are pregnant or gravely ill, you should not fast.)

Overall Benefits of Fasting:

- Takes away evil desires.
- Spiritual advancement
- Eliminate poison from previous meals
- Cleanses our blood
- Helps to keep sickness away
- Energizes you *Builds the will

*Note on One Meal A Day:

Sisters, do you have the energy to exercise three times a day for several hours each session? (I'm also talking to myself). No? Well, what makes you think your stomach has the energy to digest food several times a day when it takes more than several hours to digest a meal? There are kidney transplants and even heart transplants, but no stomach transplants. Once you wear out your stomach, that is it. Point? Eat one meal a day and give your stomach a wonderful rest. (Smile).

*Read Study Guide #13: "The Price of Redemption". It has an excellent explanation on fasting and one meal a day.

Chapter 5

Mental Health And Dis-ease

Not only does our food affect our health, but our thoughts also. In *How To Eat To Live-Book II*, it states:

> We can eat the best food, we can take fasts for i: 3 days or for 20 or 30 days if we want to: and we will still suffer if we do not feed the brain with the right food.

Some people have been able to make a direct correlation between mental health and physical health. In the book *You Can Heal Your Life* by Louise L. Hay, she gives some examples of how negative mental thoughts can lead to certain physical conditions. Here are a few that I found interesting:

- Headaches and abdominal cramps may be related to fear.
- Acne may be caused by the feelings of not liking self.
- Back pain may be associated with financial problems or lack of emotional support.
- Obesity could be related to the desire to protect self or hide anger.
- Female problems such as cysts and fibroids may be related to the denial of self or nursing a hurt.
- Knee problems may indicate a stubborn ego.
- And neck problems may signal inflexibility.

As Minister Farrakhan says, in order to <u>stay healthy</u>, we must <u>stay connected</u> with Allah(God).

Chapter 6

Energize With Exercise

Movement, movement, movement. Someone gave exercise a bad name. Sisters, we can and easily will gain weight eating one meal a day because our metabolism slows down because of the reduction of meals. If we are not exercising we are going to gain weight.

Exercise!? "I hate to exercise." Or some may say, "I don't have time to exercise." Don't look at exercise as a chore. As I mentioned earlier, movement is a joy and it is therapeutic. Different exercises, such as aerobics, running, cycling, martial arts, and dancing helps to relieve stress. The key is finding a form of movement or exercise that you like. If you don't like a particular food, you probably won't cook it very often for dinner. The same principle can be applied to exercise. If you don't like to run or get on a stair climbing machine, guess what? You probably won't exercise very often. When I'm not in the "spirit" to exercise, but I know I need to, I put on some African music or one of my favorite R & B songs and start to dance. Talk about instant upliftment. I "jam" for at least 20-25 minutes and then would move on into my weight lifting routine.

The Best Exercise
There are three types of exercises that I'm certain I will never tire of: kickboxing, dancing and walking. Sisters, do you know which exercise Minister Farrakhan said is the best exercise for us? Walking. Walking is also good for our heart and soul.

Benefits of Exercising and weight training:

- Reduces anxiety and stress
- Increases strength and endurance
- Improves bone thickness, strength and health
- Lowers blood cholesterol
- Reduces your chances of being afflicted with certain diseases
- Metabolism
- Gives you more energy
- Gives you a beautiful healthy body by reducing fat *(Fitness Theory And Practice12)*

Exercise Excuses

Now that you know the benefits of exercise, let's deal with the excuses, and eliminate or "bust them up!"

Excuses - "Whoop! There It Is!"

#1 - "I don't like to exercise."
Tough. Well, some things we have to do because they are good ior us. As I mentioned earlier, find a movement or exercise that you like. If all else fails, walk. According to the 1999 Health Magazine's Women's Health Guide, the best way to lose weight can be summed up in six words: walk briskly 45 minutes a day. It's easy and something you can do almost everyday. (I personally like to jog or take walks while listening to a Minister Farrakhan or a Sister Ava Muhammad tape. You may want to order an audiobook of your favorite author and "listen" to a couple of chapters a day. Time will fly by.)

#2 - "I have young children that allow little time for exercise."
Take your child for a walk with you or schedule a workout around one of child's naps. Between naps, you should be able to fit in at least two 15 minute or longer sessions of exercise. If the children are older, include them in your dance workout. Purchase an exercise bike and read or watch a TV show (no soap operas, please) while you ride and they nap or do homework. You may also buy a jump rope or other equipment your children can safely use and introduce them to fitness. (Some of our children are starting to look obese.)

#3 - "I don't have money for a gym membership."
See response to Excuse #1. Walking is the best and it's cheap. There are also a lot of reasonably priced videos available.

#4 - "I find it hard to motivate myself to exercise."
Team up with at least two other sisters that have similar goals. If one isn't able to exercise one day, you will always have a back-up.

#5 - "I'm already skinny. I don't need to exercise."
Exercise is not just for losing weight. It is also good for cardiovascular conditioning (our heart) and improves circulation. (If you eat a great deal and never gain weight, then you have either been blessed with a marvelous metabolic rate or you may have parasites living in your body. Check it out.)

#6 - "I'm always too tired to exercise."
Exercising will actually give you more energy. Put on some music and dance or do some jumping jacks. You won't want to stop.

#7 - "I'm too old or too big to exercise."

You are never too old to do some type of exercise. If you are very overweight, the exercising will make you feel better about yourself. If you are not ready to die, you are not too u to exercise. (Please consult a doctor before starting any type of exercise program. If you don't know how to start, you may want to invest in a personal trainer if your finances allow you that benefit.)

If there is an excuse that I haven't covered, seek refuge in Allah(God) for help. After all, He is the Best Knower.

Three additional points:
1. Don't procrastinate, just do it.
2. Think positive.
3. Be thankful.

It's impossible to be <u>depressed</u> and <u>thankful</u> at the same time. When you are thankful, you feel better about yourself and want to do things that are good for you. Have you ever noticed that the days you are not feeling good about yourself are the days you don't comb your hair or take time to dress nicely. You think, "I'll just throw a headpiece on or a hat; I don't like my looks anyway." We shouldn't constantly voice our displeasure over our weight and looks. It shows a lack of gratitude.

Sisters, we need to stop complaining, because "age ain't nothing but a number." We have a God that can help in reducing the aging process if we would just follow his instructions. (Look at Minister Louis Farrakhan.) As for our fat? "Oh, ye of little faith." Who is better at fulfilling promises but Allah? Since he created the heavens and the earth, the sun and the stars, don't you think he can help us create a healthy body and rid us of excess baggage? Sisters-- think good, feel good and do good.

Exercises and Stretches

The following exercise and stretches are from my personal routine, but I tried to pick ones almost anyone can do. Keep in mind:

- All exercises are not for everyone
- Always warm up your muscles by doing 5-10 minutes of aerobic activity before stretching and beginning a routine
- Always try to support your back and keep your body in alignment
- Support your neck
- Try to do at least 6-8 repetitions of each of the following exercises
- Drink water before and after a workout

Let's go to work!

Warm-up

I usually warm up by performing 10 sidekicks, 10 front kicks and 10 back kicks on each leg. Sometimes I may add squats to help warm up the large muscles of the legs or jumping jacks. When I am in the gym, I ride for 10-20 minutes on the bike as a warm-up.

Stretches

At the beginning of a workout, you may hold stretches for about 10 seconds. At the end of the workout, hold a stretch for 20-30 seconds to increase flexibility. Don't hold your breath or bounce during a stretch. If you force a stretch, you may injure yourself. (Also stretch your hamstrings, calves, chest, back, shoulders, arms, and neck!

Below is my favorite stretch for my quadriceps. You may use a chair for balance.

Squats and Lunges

These two exercises are excellent for the thighs quadricep and back of the thighs (the hamstrings). I usually do 27 of 10 repetitions on each leg. Make sure you support your back and don't let your knee go past your toes in each exercise. These exercises help to strengthen and tone your legs into lovely extensions of your lower body.

Military Press

For shapely shoulders, try military presses. Try to invest in a pair of 3-5 pound dumbbells for a beginner's workout. Breathe out as you push the dumbbells up and breathe in when you lower the weight.

Lateral Raise

Start with dumbbells lowered in front of you and lift un ar raise them to shoulder level. This exercise shapes your upper shoulders which makes your waist appear smaller.

Push-up

The push-up works your chest and triceps muscles. It is a great upper body exercise you can do when you get up in the morning. Keep your body in alignment by not arching your hack. You may do the push-up on your knees or toes.

Bicep Curls

This exercise works the bicep muscles. You raise both arms at the same time or alternate arms. We all need some type of weight training or our muscles will atrophy (waste away). We don't want to be skinny weaklings, do we?

Back

No, I am not trying to be Superwoman or practice flying. The top picture is a back strengthening exercise. Lie prone (on your stomach and look at the floor, not at the camera like me) and raise your opposite arm and leg at the same time. Hold for 5-10 seconds and then switch. After this exercise, you should form a modified cobra stretch which is a yoga move.
(Dr. Phulgenda Sinha, a master teacher of yoga, said the full cobra yoga stretch helps Condition and massage the lower internal organs.)